Sweet Land

poems by

Sherry Siddall

Finishing Line Press
Georgetown, Kentucky

Sweet Land

Copyright © 2021 by Sherry Siddall
ISBN 978-1-64662-619-9 First Edition
All rights reserved under International and Pan-American Copyright Conventions. No part of this book may be reproduced in any manner whatsoever without written permission from the publisher, except in the case of brief quotations embodied in critical articles and reviews.

ACKNOWLEDGMENTS

Landscaping, *Kakalak*, 2020
Oysters, *Kakalak*, 2019
Tell Everyone On This Train I Love Them, *Tar River Poetry*, Spring 2018
Cross Quarter Day, *Kakalak*, 2018
Early Spring, *Kakalak*, 2016
Daphne Odora, *Kakalak* 2015
Let Us Know the Night, *Pinesong*, 2017, Joanna Catherine Scott Award and Poetry in Plain Sight, 2021
The Pink Dogwood, My Green Rumpled Field, *Tar River Poetry*, Spring 2014

Publisher: Leah Huete de Maines
Editor: Christen Kincaid
Cover Art: Sherry Siddall
Author Photo: Sherry Siddall
Cover Design: Elizabeth Maines McCleavy

Order online: www.finishinglinepress.com
also available on amazon.com

Author inquiries and mail orders:
Finishing Line Press
PO Box 1626
Georgetown, Kentucky 40324
USA

Table of Contents

- Let Us Know the Night 1
- Oysters 2
- Ark 3
- Petrichor 5
- Before the Frost 6
- Cardinal 7
- Loud January 8
- February, 1965 9
- Daphne Odora 10
- Early Spring 11
- Daffodils 12
- "Tell Everyone on This Train I Love Them" 13
- Cross Quarter Day 14
- New Growth 15
- Mock Orange 16
- Elegy 17
- Sheltering in Place 18
- Perseids 19
- Sweet Land 20
- Monarchs 21
- Terns 22
- Coyote 23
- Drought 24
- Revelation 25
- Landscaping 26
- Weeds 27
- My Green Rumpled Field 28
- Pamlico Portrait 29
- Hunting Season 30
- The Move 31
- Ashes 32
- The Waters of Grief 33
- Night Sky 34

Dedicated to the Memory of
Eric Townsend Brigham 1918-1965
and
John Brane Siddall 1927-2014

Let Us Know the Night

At sunset geese have settled in the field
close by the spring fed pond, dark water green.
Mock orange newly blown, its white blooms yield
a quiet scent that fills the air, unseen.

The dogs smell deer, run barking to the fence.
What cannot be contained, the weedy roar,
bees who rub themselves against the blooms, sense
time is short before the moon decants its pour

of milky light, a cataract of sleep
that folds all in, suspends the drive to find
the perfect food, the perfect love, the deep
connection where we leave the past behind.

Let us not be lost as dark descends.
Let us know the night, its comfort and its end.

Oysters

My husband opens
oysters for me
on my birthday.
Shucks them.

One by one he
finds the spot
where the knife
will slide, severs
flesh from its
muscled hinge,
cracks open
the adamant shell,
ridged and whorled
hard as a fossil
to reveal a cool
briny creature,
its smooth salty flesh
a revelation.

He places each half shell
on my plate for me to savor
the simplest, most perfect
gift.

Ark

Walking on the beach I find a jingle shell,
near dune's edge the chalky buttercups.
Imagine Noah loading his ponderous ark
with earth's large creatures screeching in tongues
but forgetting the lettered olives, lion's paws, hawk wings,
flushed by the tides in their sea bubble.

Before the rains came, magma bubbled,
mountains exploded through the earth's shell.
The winds subsided and birds spread their wings,
Each nest building the soil until buttercups
appeared one day, yellow and delicious on the tongue.
Adam and Eve arose together, their bodies an ark

whose children flourish now, follow the rainbow's arc
over oceans, where schools of fish send bubbles
foaming over waves, minnows tickling like tongues
on the legs of children gathering shells.
They run to their mothers, glowing like buttercups,
shedding their towels like wings.

Overhead birds screech and dive, winging
a route over white-capped waves that arch
and roll as the sun's flattened buttercup
melts in the sea, as once again the dark bubble
of earth holds us intact in the galaxy's shell,
where animals in our dreams are speaking in tongues.

In the northern forest a bear's sandpaper tongue
gives a lick to her cub, who's ready to spread his wings,
emerge from his dark den, winter's stuffy shell,
tumble out the way cubs do, fish for salmon in the river's arc
where it rushes over rocks, churning and bubbling
between its banks where Spring has driven up the buttercups.

In the cities there are no bears, no buttercups.
Waves of people flow up and down the sidewalks, tongues
speak into phones, feet move, minds caught in a bubble.
They'd like to escape their disconnected lives, hobbled wings
that keep them from returning to forgotten arks,
sanctuaries safe from the brain's artillery of mortar shells.

I still hear tongues of the ocean in every empty shell
hope for fields awash in buttercups come the bubble of Spring
watch for a dove approaching the ark in a flutter of wings.

Petrichor

travels on the wind
ushering rain.
This green smell
blood of the rock
fluid in the veins
of gods
decaying matter
transformed
exhales
its warm breath
announcing the rain
blossoming
at our feet.

Gods we are not
but still delight
as the earth sighs
with pleasure
when rain caresses
dry ground aching
from drought.
We are part of it
still alive
still breathing deeply
inhaling
these smallest particles
we will someday become.

Before the Frost

In the health care wing
light plays over your soft form
as leaves of memory fall

become those photos
where faces unremembered
out of context go

almost unremarked
one by one, so painlessly
they depart, you smile

say, *I never thought
it would come to this*, surprised
to feel no chill

before the frost, just
a thrilling of crickets chanting
beneath fallen leaves

the sun unburdened
of heat, spent knowledge sharing
its long gift, a life

well lived and constant
in its warmth, future solstice
just the sun's turning…

winter is coming
it will be glorious soon, all
the light absorbed, done.

Cardinal

Winter morning sees the mock orange
stripped of leaves by a north wind.
Dry branches cradle a skeleton nest,
brush stroke of a former life,
summer's sere negative.

At noon, a luminous cardinal
lights among the tangle,
black eye fervent as an evangelist,
beating heart, candescent red,
the only spot of color anywhere.

Now at dusk his presence
pierces winter's heart.
Wind blowing, sun gone,
he glows, impossibly alive
as darkness overwhelms.

Loud January

The wind blows stiffly,
diminishing a Buddha sun.

I offer my face, hands, observe
the sparkle on the pond.

There are gun shots too,
a mile away or more

blasting fast and hard, then
slowing, waiting, stopped.

I hear fierce birds again,
as a brown horse watches me

over the fence. He's just
making sure I am what I seem

before cantering away, hooves
thumping deep on wet pasture.

Faintly, a hammer rings across
the pond, an unlatched barn door

swings shut, open, shut, open, though
it makes no sound that I can hear.

February, 1965

It is strange to see the hospital bed
in the front bedroom, flooded with sunlight
and you lying there, without speech,
where cancer has left you.

I have come home after school, Mother
still at work, a cold sunny February day
where chickadees flock the feeder
and a nurse watches TV in another room.

Why have they left you alone this way
like a sea creature stranded by the tide?
Perhaps it wasn't so, just what I recall,
the two of us, your life fast receding.

I'm telling you about my day when you
grab my hand, your jaundiced eyes
locking onto mine. Although your voice
is gone, your eyes speak years.

Forgive me, they say, *I want to stay.*
What I remember is the strength
of your grip, the sadness you felt
at leaving, that overwhelming tide.

Daphne Odora

How can I describe this fragrance?

It is the Chinese emperor arriving in heaven
with chariots and concubines.

It is the perfume of the unicorn's mane
billowing in mythical gallop.

It is my mother's corsage on Easter Sunday
gracing the lapel of her tailored suit.

It is my father's pillow. He is a child
dreaming of adventure.

There is no death, no future, only the glorious
plundering scent of memory, which is now.

Early Spring

Palsied beech leaves release
their winter grip.

I have thrown down the dried nest
from the weathered house, brittle and empty

awaiting a mated pair of blue birds,
shocking in their color, their urgency.

It was such a long winter
and cold, the wind beseeching

the way the elderly do
with their eyes when speech is gone,

their need as strong as that wind,
as prescient as the blue mated pair.

Daffodils

Sepia tones, the baby
holds up both hands

all gone!
The house is too,

but daffodils still
play peek-a-boo.

They follow a sweet rain,
a pattering childhood rain

that washed us to sleep
elsewhere.

Now the greenest grass
is over the septic field

where the beds pop up
untended every year,

expecting a house,
the baby, leaving us

an earthy grief,
missing the tenders

who went somewhere
without their cameras.

"Tell Everyone On This Train I Love Them"
For Taliesin Myrddin Namkai-Meche and Rachel Macy
May 26, 2017

His final words to the woman who stayed to comfort him.
A single mother of five who removed her black tank top
to staunch his blood, covered his hand with hers.
He said, "I'm going to die." She looked at him and said,
"We can handle this. Lay down."

Minutes before on the packed train three men stood between
two frightened girls and the ranting man with the knife, tried
to divert his meteoric rage with soothing words. Only one survived
what happened next, three rapid strikes as the train arrived, one fell
and died, one staggered, one fled as the car swiftly emptied of life.

She spoke to him as a mother speaks to a beloved child.
"You're such a beautiful man. I'm sorry the world
is so cruel…" And she prayed while he closed his eyes,
tried to keep breathing. When the medics carried him
away, he spoke his charge to her, "tell everyone…"

She stayed, answering their questions in her bloodied slip
until word came that he had died, until an officer said,
"You did what you could, it's time to come off the train."
How do you get off the train? How do you handle this
when love has sent you down that fearsome track?

Cross Quarter Day

The redwing's throaty trill
      is one that makes me think
           of summer fields, of heat
and blowing grain.
      Yet here they are on this first
           cross quarter day between solstice
                and equinox, not quite winter,
not quite spring. Where the staff of
      a goddess tapped the earth,
           told it to waken, brought the ewes
in milk. Who has told the blackbirds?
      Rowdy on the dormant trees
           they seem to know
winter won't last,
         as does the brown hawk
              atop the well house
who watches them
      with jaded eye as the flock
           rises in cacophony of
have you heard the news?
      settles back with raucous
           chatter, pausing on the way
to spring. As I pass
      all go silent. When did I become
           winter's dark angel?

New Growth

First week of April every year
the leaves emerge in one bright push.

Where bareness crackled there is softness,
fast unfurling curls, each practiced leaf

transforms its living branch, Earth's
green fontanelle, revealing itself again.

Even a grounded log, sliced from a maple
felled last fall, is sprouting limber shoots,

delicate buds owning no root, no source
but this solid length, having suffered the final cut

and wintered over, no future here, no joy,
but still those buds.

Mock Orange

I've written about this bush
in winter, bare ribbed skeleton

surrounding the red cardinal,
tangled twigs holding ground.

How in winter this red bird
anchored all, the shrub itself

a prop, a back drop. Now
in April this plant alive, tall

and densely green, white blossoms
thick and simple, heavy on those

same dry twigs gone supple,
arching, beckoning in fragrant voice,

the same bush, the very same
where the cardinal waited in winter rain.

Elegy

I found the red cardinal
dead beneath my window.

His limp head, the sunken
blackness of his eye said death,

yet his body bright as flame was soft
above his fanned stiff tail.

For two winters in all weather
he visited the bare whips of wood,

the mock orange that would be lithe
and scented come spring. He perched

in the middle, spending his redness
when there was no color,

no verse but coming dark.
I held the last gift of his body,

laid him at the roots of that bush
soon to bloom again.

Sheltering in Place

The wren built her nest
in the lattice roof
of the screened porch,
crafted it twig by twig.

I propped the door open
with a granite stone
so she could fly at will
to nurture her brood.

She fussed at me
from the snowbell tree,
heavy with white blooms,
as I ate my lunch nearby.

I didn't mind. All was busy
and hopeful as she dipped
in and out, knowing what to do,
until one night late

I saw her huddled
against the house, back
feathers ruffled, alive but still.
In the morning she was gone

and there was the snake, lazy
coils of bulging body hanging
from lattice. When I tried
to make it fall, make it leave

the snake retreated, lunging
at the broom, tongue flickering,
to a darker hiding place above,
just near the ruined nest.

The porch is quiet now, door
still open in hope the snake will go.
As for the wren, I need to believe
she lives to nest again.

Perseids
> *For Geoffrey*

There are no storms tonight
and the stars are sending
messages of light
from long ago

Tomorrow is your day
of dust to dust
when I will free your ashes
in newly turned ground

Your voice is still
on the answering machine
Its gruff hello and
my nickname.

Now there is no one left
who knows the story
or will call me
by this silly name.

The stars are blind
to kindness, which was
your legacy to me,
forgiveness your gift.

In fact, your life was
oxygen to my lungs.
I wish I had told you this
before.

Brother whose life anchored mine
May your soul be freer than
a message of light, sent to
awe us on this August night.

Sweet Land

When Mary Oliver walked
she saw a fawn with its mother
a snake sunning itself
the fur of a rabbit
beside a holy stream.

The image I see this week,
a scrolling brown river
neutral in grace, where
father and daughter float
face down in locked embrace.

At border checkpoints the living
surrender their water, their
children, enter the holding pens,
silver mylar blankets
crackling like angel wings.

In the land of the free it's a holiday.
A tank display on the National Mall
celebrates brutality, as the POTUS
speaks to the chosen in chairs
behind ropes, rain, bulletproof glass.

I watch TV with the sound off,
scroll on my phone, hope to see
a fawn with its mother or a snake
sunning itself. Even the fur of the rabbit
would be welcome.

Monarchs

They arrive in February, searching for milkweed,
that magic plant from childhood. Nursery
for egg, caterpillar and chrysalis. Ten days
from pupa to butterfly, two weeks to die.

Repeat three times. By August, reincarnate,
they are everywhere, bobbing lightly on zinnias
labeled "cut and come again", from seeds we
scattered blithely only weeks ago.

Each flower face is milked of nectar, its sustenance
the lightest food we can imagine. Powdery wings
fan open in yellow and black, injured,
incomplete, focused on the short time here.

A smiling orange flower, brief respite
before the slipstream of heat and wind sucks
even the most determined down to the
black tar of ending.

Released and reborn from their milkweed homes
three times before the spell breaks. A fourth
generation is driven by the call south,
the far mountains of Michoacan.

Thousands of miles find them thick
in the mountains of Mexico, warm breeze
caressing their wings, no memory
of all that came before.

Terns

Hundreds in unison, this choir's
mute arpeggio high above
the going nowhere dock,
where each shift and flow shows
specks of gray or brilliant white
moving as one when westering light
catches the dip and glide each side.

A gossamer scarf thrown casually,
reluctant to land, convulses
on the wind's whim.
They circle then settle on the dock,
merely a flock of birds
waiting for the front to pass.

Coyote

When snow covered the pond, the road, the field,
a coyote stole the orange barn cat, whom we loved.
A friendly cat who rubbed her body softly
against our legs, rolled over for a scratch,
slept nightly with the old horse in his heated stall.

My neighbor saw it crossing the field
behind the barn in full daylight, twitchy, alert,
hungry perhaps, with pups to feed. We saw
the pelts of small animals dark against the snow,
and the cat gone, no sign anywhere.

We heard their yips, carried sticks while walking,
brought the dogs inside, never thought of ourselves
as predator or prey. We closed our doors
in this suburban neighborhood, called Animal Control
to trap and kill, no relocation here.

While we mulled who lives or dies, after five days
the cat returned, resumed her place in the horse's stall.
The coyote still at large, and doing what
coyotes do, we're back to wondering why we must
exterminate all who threaten us.

Drought

In June the caterpillars feasted
on sweet leaves of the ornamental
bush, stripped it so fast
you could hear their jaws working.

What is that crunching sound?
Death dealing or life giving,
depending on your point of view.
Manna to this bloom of chompers

who moved on in their life cycle
as the bush pushed out new leaves,
smaller than before, but true,
a second coming of sorts.

Wilting now from a rainless month
of heat, it suffers again.
Lank leaves droop on arching stems
as the season empties itself.

I drag the green hose to water it
laying the stream at its roots,
where a sort of miracle occurs as
the leaves respond, willing to try again.

Everything around me waits for rain.
So far I am the lucky one
who turns the spigot on and off, who
lets the water flow, who drinks at will.

Revelation

The world has stopped
for all of us
whether we agree
or disagree

huddling alone
or with those we love
inside or outside
but always apart.

Smog over cities
drifts away, revealing
sharp blue mountains
that were always there.

Fish glide freely
among anchored boats,
skies alive with boisterous birds
who suddenly own the air.

Yet still an echoing
emptiness everywhere
except for the coming
of Spring, green and grinning.

The new virus, invisible as God,
has found the perfect host
in us, who have always taken
anything we wanted.

Now, it takes us.

Landscaping

Today I noticed the pine
    that was a shoot
I could pull up with my hands
    is now a sapling with a backbone
and a mind of its own.
    Today's garden, tomorrow's wood.
What looks to be a winding vine
    has sent green fingers everywhere.
informing the dirt with vein-like roots.
    Weed as I will, it will have its way.
Which is good to know, because
    when we have destroyed ourselves
and everything we love, when the fires
    have burned themselves out
and nothing is left but swarming insects
    and polluted springs
there will be vines twining their limbs over
    concrete ruins, walking a green blanket
over our only Eden and its bones.

Weeds

The weeds I pull this morning
lie wilting on the grass.
Tendrils of morning glory wither
with stiltgrass, spurge
and those nameless things
I have decided will never bloom.

These weeds grow fiercely.
Their roots grab the earth as I tug
regardless of delicate neighbors
who need light and space.
What are labels? Who's to say
this plant is good, this one bad?

I am the god of labels. I have decided.
The limp fading pile of sad green
speaks to this, proclaims me
emperor of my narrow plot.
The rainforest burns, life is erased.
Someone has decided.

My Green Rumpled Field

seems almost to move
with the sound of crickets,

the ladybug on my finger
wise from listening.

The light is long and earnest,
young the way Spring is young,

Yellow butterflies bob and duck
across the rolling green.

Here the clover believes
it has always been here,

always been illuminated
by the sideways light

that glows right through
so anyone could see

the velvet underside
thin veins and furred stems,

the field quivering with wind and light
the ladybug crawling on my hand

like a confused ruby.

Pamlico Portrait

At day's end keeping company
with a ruffled statesman,

Great Blue, stoic on his bulkhead,
stretches one leg, faultless, still.

A pair of ducks cruise on chuckled water,
family grown or fated otherwise,

the long dock thick with waiting gulls
strangely quiet.

Rhythmic laps from the last boat
shuffle needle grass, cedar bones.

Young egret strolls the matted
wrack alive with food.

Overhead a clacking armada of geese,
one pelican crabbing sideways on the wind.

Gathering in the north, a cloud bank tinged
with steel writes an elegy on the failing light.

Hunting Season

At dawn they fly into the sun,
fall like Icarus one by one,
feathered necks bowed to shotgun blast,
birdshot screaming past.

All day the intermittent booms
echo across the Sound, a room
of bruising silence over shattered water.
Life in the marsh, not slaughter.

Practical ducks drift, the tide in spate,
dipping to fish, gliding with mates.
One vivid male carves the cove, his band
of females follows in a swirling fan.

Afternoon, wind lapses, water calms.
The brittle sun shines a psalm
over marsh and creaking geese
go clacking past. A strange peace.

Meanwhile, hunters crowd
the taco stand, trucks idling loud,
order beef burritos with a beer,
brag on birds bagged, speak of deer.

At dusk, limp feathered bodies line a rail,
graceful in death, oddly free, they fail
to offer more than meat, lie without care
near camo waders draped to air.

The Move

You were cheerful when we talked.
Every few months the phone would ring,
big brother here, at seventy-four
still taking the bus to work, most days.

Now in your dark house, light struggles
to get in or out, strangled houseplants die
in macramé hangers. Proud, you wouldn't
want me here, trash bags in hand.

In your room, drawers on the floor, boxes
of new shirts, 16/34. Perks of working
at The Shop, until this habit failed you,
your body busy, shutting down.

In one corner live the plastic bags
of dirty clothes rising to consume
immaculate jackets in the narrow closet,
pressed trousers asleep in their filmy bags.

I picture you in the dining room sorting
a pile of gloves, frustrated by their
lack of mates, thinking the fault yours,
spending hours doing this.

In the bathroom ragged towels, empty
bottles of imported cologne, and
under the sink, the dregs of a fifth,
your timing just exactly right.

Turning the sad mattress looking for clues,
how did I miss the wind-up to that evening
when you walked out the door, wearing only
two snappy shirts and your underwear?

Ashes

The mailman hands me your ashes
on this sunny end of summer day.

The box is heavy, which surprises me.
These ashes are not soft like moth wings

smeared upon a cheek, or crossed
upon the forehead during Lent.

These ashes are the pumice of bones,
when dementia held you in its fist,

scoured the inside of your skull
until, at the end, you saw me not at all.

Brother, this is our own dust to dust.
No more snowmen in rough New England.

No more seek me in the dark as I count to ten.
We were much to each other, even then.

Cleaning out your place, I find that sweater
I knit for you long ago, unworn but kept,

I let it go. Remembering aside, I hold
what's left of you in my two hands.

The Waters of Grief

At first, I thought I could swim
head above water, eye on the shore.
Like my dog intent on the ball
eyes focused, legs paddling hard.
It wasn't like that.

I thought of dipping my toes,
wading ankle deep in waters I knew
could swallow me. Day by day
I approached, backed away.
Of course it was too late.

I was underwater long before I knew
the drill, *turn around don't drown,*
swept sideways by the water
on my road. Deceptive, it looked
like I could walk across unscathed.

Now I'm trying a different way,
filling my cup with manageable drafts,
sipping a little bit each day,
thinking, it will take more than one
lifetime to drink it all.

Night Sky

The stars hang vivid tonight,
tucked in the black mantle of space,
cold and looming with its bite
of emptiness, all life erased.

In an open field we see these stars above
the glow from town, its determined cast
holding back the dark with light like love
but not. Look up in wonder, awe, at last

recalling those who passed before,
sending their light to that black sphere
that swallows every love outpoured,
its swirl of vastness pressing near.

None of earth's beauty holds us so fast
as this sky, this immensity flying past.

www.ingramcontent.com/pod-product-compliance
Lightning Source LLC
LaVergne TN
LVHW041557070426
835507LV00011B/1147